Presented to

....

By

....

On This Da

....

QUIET
WHISPERS
FROM
God's
Heart
FOR COUPLES

DAVID &
CLAUDIA ARP

In the beginning God created man. He created them male and female. He created them in His image. And to this day a husband and a wife who love God and love each other can reflect God's image to a hurting and broken world. You can be such a couple if you learn to listen and follow the quiet whispers from God's heart to yours.

Perhaps you've felt His presence—that gentle nudge, an impression, a soft reminder . . . almost an audible whisper from the very heart of God that helped you refocus and renew your love and commitment to each other.

We believe that if we really listen with our hearts . . . we can hear His quiet whispers in our everyday experiences. That's what this little book is all about— learning to discern God's voice and following His leading.

Won't you join us as together we view a kaleido- scope of loving couples who, in the midst of their joy and pain, learned to hear God's gentle whispers? Our prayer is that in the quietness of your heart you, too, will hear His voice—that you will experience God's touch and reflect His love to those around you.

DAVID AND CLAUDIA ARP
AUGUST 1999

CONTENTS

Weddings . . . times of celebration, times of joy, and times of new beginnings. Each wedding is special, but this particular wedding, for us, was unique. Rachel and Cannon were to be married under a canopy. The canopy, taken from the Jewish wedding tradition, signified God's protective covering for the bridal pair. Flowers and ribbon graciously adorned the tulle canopy under which the couple would soon stand to take their vows.

Rachel, strikingly beautiful in her elegant yet simple wedding dress, floated down the aisle on her father's arm. In just a few moments her father would perform the role of clergyman and lead the ceremony.

He brought me to the banqueting house, and his banner over me was love.

SONG OF SONGS 2:4

We had known Rachel for many years and had watched her grow up and transition through the adolescent years to womanhood. Now she was about to commit herself to love, cherish, and partner Cannon for the rest of her life.

We thought of the changes just ahead. In a few weeks Cannon would begin medical school. Their life would be hectic and full–very, very full. We prayed silently that God's canopy of love would protect them; that God would guide them; that they would remain faithful to the vows they were about to take.

Then a gentle nudge came from God's heart . . . *Pray too for your own marriage and the other marriages represented here today. Pray that those who have been given this trust of marriage might prove faithful. Pray that you will keep living out your marriage under My holy canopy day by day.*

A CONSTANT LOVE

I t's early morning on a spring day. The sun's rays are quickly chasing off the fog. The water in the bubbling brook and the wild flowers peeking through the snow greet two hikers. They are college students, desperately in love, cherishing precious moments alone together. Following the Smokey Mountain trail up and down the hills, they attack the rough terrain, while in the valley below the brook widens and the musical sound of the rustling water fills the air. The majestic mountains tower above.

The lovers stop frequently to embrace. At the trail's end the boisterous water leaps over Abrams Falls and drowns out the couple's concerns and fears. Hand in hand they pledge their love: *Our love for each other will flow just as constantly as this waterfall for as long as we both shall live.*

Leap forward four decades. Years have passed, but the path to Abrams Falls is unchanged. It's another beautiful spring day. The lovers on the path are now grandparents—card-carrying AARP members. They walk more slowly but just as intentionally. Hand in hand, they steady each other over the rough places. Years of the trials of living have gone by, but still in love they slowly traverse the hills and valleys. Stopping to rest, they embrace. They kiss and remember stolen kisses here on this path so many years ago.

Once again they listen to the roar of Abrams Falls. They watch the sparkling water cascade over the rocks, smooth from centuries of contact. So much in life has changed, yet Abrams Falls seems the same. The same rocks, the same towering mountains, the same path, the same rushing water, the same peace.

You are always new. The last of your kisses was ever the sweetest.

JOHN KEATS

Suddenly, they realize they are standing on holy ground. Reverently they listen, and their Heavenly Father, the Creator of Abrams Falls, the Creator of love, speaks in a whisper to their hearts: *The beauty of nature and the ability to love is My gift to you. Your love, which has endured the rapids and waterfalls of life, is your gift back to Me. Embrace. Kiss. Cherish and celebrate your love in the afternoon of your lives.*

Quiet Whispers from God's Heart for Couples

The honeymoon suite was romantic, complete with heart-shaped spa and a dozen red roses. Definitely a great setting for our twentieth-anniversary celebration. But it was not to be—at least not on this particular anniversary.

We took one last longing glance at the room just waiting for us to enjoy, grabbed the vase of roses, closed the door, and got back in our car. Then we drove the hour back home. Our youngest son had come down with the flu.

Later that evening as we munched our anniversary pizza, we remember how years ago we had pledged to love each other in sickness and in health. We were so young. I (Claudia) was barely twenty. Dave was twenty-two. Two college students, desperately in love . . . and afraid. Khrushchev was going to blow the world up. It was during the Cuban missile crisis. We were afraid we would never get to live together as husband and wife. So we did it. We got married right in the middle of college.

Well, the world didn't blow up, and over the years, we've had many opportunities to love each other in sickness and in health—both our illnesses and those of our three sons! And here we were again . . . another disappointment. More cancelled plans.

Another opportunity to live out our marriage vows. And then we realized . . . *That's what marriage is all about—supporting and loving each other when things work out and when things don't work out. We had vowed to be there for each other in sickness and in health, for richer or for poorer, and for better or for worse.*

Marriage is a package deal. The good comes with the bad. Health, sickness, times of abundance, times of need, times things are great, times things are lousy—all are part of the fabric of marriage. And while it's much more enjoyable to love in health than in sickness, both are vital if we want to have a growing, and lasting marriage.

So on that anniversary, home with our sick son, we informally renewed our vows. We looked at our roses, cuddled on the couch, and slipped a video in the VCR. Perhaps next year we'd try again for the heart-shaped spa. Meanwhile, we would love each other in sickness and in health.

There is surely a future hope for you, and your hope will not be cut off.

PROVERBS 23:18

Quiet Whispers from God's Heart for Couples

He is the love of my life and I know I'm the love of his," Ruby said. "But my husband rarely expresses his love in words. Basically, I say it and Ralph thinks it."

"Does this bother you?" we asked.

"Not really," Ruby replied. "I decided a long time ago that I didn't want to miss connecting to him just because I'm a talker and he's not, so I don't nag him or demand a lot of talk. I try to enjoy the shared silence."

Ruby speaks from experience. She and Ralph just celebrated their twenty-fifth wedding anniversary—twenty-five years of marriage history.

My heart is ever at your service.

WILLIAM SHAKESPEARE

In their early twenties they started a trucking business. Before the kids came along, they trucked together. "We would go for miles and miles, and Ralph would say nothing," Ruby said. "At first it bothered me. I'd bait him for compliments and conversations, but the more I persisted, the quieter he became. Long periods of ice-cold silence. Each of us was missing the other's expectations. Then one day it hit me: *Listen to his heart—don't demand his words.*"

As we listened to Ruby, we thought, *What difference would it make in our own marriage, if we concentrated on listening to each other's heart and not emphasizing the words or lack of them?*

Would we give each other the benefit of the doubt? Would we express our love in non-verbal ways—a glance across the room, a hug, or kiss? Would we seek to affirm the other, instead of waiting for the other's affirmation? What would happen if, just for today, we listened to each other's heart?

Quiet Whispers from God's Heart for Couples

The rays of the sun danced on the pristine snow as the gondola rose higher and higher. All was quiet, except for an occasional thump as we passed under another supporting tower. Below us, majestic evergreens laden with snow bowed silently in reverence.

Reaching the summit, we disembarked. A breathtaking panorama of the majestic Austrian Alps surrounded us. We felt as though we were standing on holy ground.

But the spell was broken when I (Claudia) said, "Dave, how are we going to get back down to the bottom? It's so steep!"

"Obviously," Dave answered, "we're going to ski down. After all, that's why we took the twenty-minute gondola ride."

Years ago, skiing had been our family's favorite sport—but that was years ago. Now, we were venturing out once again. Out of practice, our ski legs—though weak—were determined to hit the slopes . . . as long as we hit them slowly.

It seemed a perfect day for skiing. Swish! Swish! We began our descent, stopping often to enjoy the beauty of it all. And with each successful turn, we became more confident—until halfway down the mountain we ran into fog! Thick fog. Pea-soup fog. This was not part of our plan! Pleasure was replaced with panic.

Glorify the Lord with me; let us exalt his name together.

PSALM 34:3

"What are we going do to now?" I asked.

Clueless, Dave answered, "Pray."

Together we considered our options. We could sidestep down, but in the thick fog others might crash into us. We could take off our skis and walk down, but even then, not knowing the slope, we might get lost.

As we wrestled with our options, another couple, skiing at about our pace, passed by and stopped just below us. Their laughter and obvious lack of concern assured us they knew the slope. They weren't gripped with fear like their two American observers. So as they skied into the fog, we bravely followed. When they turned, we turned. When they stopped to rest, we stopped to rest. Without realizing what they were doing, they guided us safely down the mountain.

Answered prayer? Definitely! Angels in ski suits? Probably not, but they could have been! Unknowingly, they had modeled for us and provided a path in the snow for us to follow. Then it struck us . . . *Others are watching us-what are we modeling?*

Quiet Whispers from God's Heart for Couples

While we aren't the best models for traversing and getting down ski slopes, we began to realize that couples may be following us in other ways. What about younger couples who pattern their marriage after ours? Or the couples in our Sunday-school class who watch how we handle difficult situations, or how we deal with conflict, or even how we handle success? Yes, others may be watching us right now and be influenced by how we relate to each other. Are we being good models?

What about you? What difference would it make if you knew others were watching you? In our confusing foggy world yours might be the only marriage model others see clearly.

It's something to think about.

F or Rick, it was just a routine check-up with the dermatologist. The doctor said that removing the small mole was preventative; there was nothing to worry about.

Then the phone call came. Would Rick come back in? The doctor could see him at 3 PM tomorrow.

The next day Rick and his wife, Joyce, sat across from the doctor. "Rick, the mole was malignant," the doctor said. "You have melanoma." He paused for a moment, then continued, "I've made an appointment for you with a surgeon. He will do some tests, and we'll go from there. We caught it early. And that's positive."

Rick and Joyce looked at each other. Positive! How could cancer ever be positive?

Numb, confused, scared, and riddled with anxiety, they listened as the doctor tried to reassure them.

Later that evening, after getting their three young children in bed, they held each other and vowed to get through this crisis together. They considered the future. What was ahead? Surgery? Radiation? Chemotherapy? Often the greatest stressor is dread— the fear of what might happen. Would the cancer spread? Would he die?

In the middle of their fears, they prayed, "God, we don't know what to do, but our eyes are upon you. Please give us your comfort and your peace and see us through this crisis."

Later that night as they read from the Book of Psalms, God comforted them and addressed their fears . . . *Even in darkness light dawns for the upright. . . . He will have no fear of bad news; his heart is steadfast, trusting in the Lord* (Ps. 112:4, 7).

In the coming weeks, Rick, with Joyce at his side, got through the surgery. The doctor removed the lymph nodes, and they prayed that the cancer had been caught in time.

At times Rick was strong. Other times he was fearful, and Joyce carried the load. Waiting several weeks for the final lab report was a dark time for both of them. Then the good news, "Your lab report came back negative," the doctor said.

Sometimes things work out well, as they did for Rick and Joyce. Other times God gives the grace and comfort to get through the bad news. If, like Rick and Joyce, you choose to focus on God and trust Him in the darkness, you don't have to live in fear. Whatever the future holds, He will see you through it. The darkness of your situation will not be so dark when you follow God's light.

The stars are constantly shining, but often we do not see them until the dark hours.

EARL RINEY

As we ate dinner with marriage enrichment pioneers David and Vera Mace, we were intrigued with the way they looked so tenderly at each other. Could a couple who had been married over forty years still have the spark?

Yes, and it was contagious! We were in the North Carolina mountains with several other couples for a week of training. As the Maces talked with the group that evening, it was almost as if the two were speaking as one.

Commit to the Lord whatever you do, and your plans will succeed.

PROVERBS 16:3

Later that night, we knew we had found a living model of what we wanted for our own marriage. Could *we* have such a vibrant marriage after we had been married for forty or fifty years? Then in a quiet whisper the answer came: *Yes, but now is the time to decide what you want your marriage to look like in the future.*

For the rest of that week we reflected on what we wanted our marriage to look like when we were in our seventies . . . our eighties . . . and, if God should grant us more years together, in our nineties. What did we want to characterize our relationship on our fiftieth wedding anniversary?

Now, almost two decades have gone by. Time for another check-up. What progress have we made? What dreams are yet to be fulfilled?

Now is the time to decide what our marriage will look like in the future!

Quiet Whispers from God's Heart for Couples

The raindrops drummed a boring cadence on the windowsill, not unlike Lucy and Philip's ho-hum relationship. Sitting across from the counselor, they knew their marriage was in trouble—filled with broken promises, missed expectations, lost dreams.

Lucy and Philip had met in college and married right before Philip started law school. Lucy put her own academic plans on hold and worked as a hotel receptionist to help Philip get through law school. But those years of hard work and struggling to make ends meet transitioned into years of affluence. Philip had just made partner in his New York law firm. To others, it appeared they were on "easy street." Then why were they so miserable?

True, their lives were opulent and affluent with things, but their relationship was impoverished. Houses, cars, and "stuff" didn't bridge the chasm in their relationship. They needed help. That's why they were here, but was it too late?

"When a long-term marriage crumbles," the counselor said, "usually it's not the result of a major crisis or a one-time event. Like your experience, little things build up over the years. It's easy to disconnect emotionally. But a relationship is much easier to put back together within the framework of a marriage. It's up to you. You can choose to reconnect, to rebuild your relationship and start over. Are you willing?"

Philip and Lucy looked at each other. Each knew the answer should be yes, but they had no emotional reserve—no strength left to verbalize it. The hurts and disappointments were deeply embedded. Could they really start over? Silently they looked at each other . . . if only they could go back years ago when they lived in poverty but their relationship was abounding in love. Slowly Philip reached for Lucy's hand. They touched . . . and suddenly there was a glimmer of hope. Was it really possible—a new beginning? Then it was as if God whispered to their hearts . . . *Yes, this can be a day of new beginnings. What is impossible with man is possible with me. I will make all things new!*

"How do we start?" Philip asked the counselor. Lucy shook her head in agreement.

"Let's start," the counselor said, "with the One who created marriage in the first place. Let's commit this process to God and ask for His guidance and help."

Forgiveness ought to be like a canceled note—torn in two, and burned up, so that it never can be shown against one.

HENRY WARD BEECHER

Quiet Whispers from God's Heart for Couples

Together they bowed their heads. "Father, we come before you this afternoon," the counselor prayed, "to ask for your strength for Philip and Lucy. Give them the courage to forgive each other, to release their hurts and disappointments, to focus on the future, and to rebuild their marriage. Now, please guide us in this process and make this a day of new beginnings."

Lucy squeezed Philip's hand. Their eyes locked. Both knew the road ahead would not be an easy one. "You don't solve in one day what took years to develop," the counselor had told them. But deep in their hearts, they knew with God's help it was possible to start over. For them, this was indeed a day of new beginnings!

At a neighborhood party, Kelly asked in frustration, "Can you tell me what a healthy marriage looks like? I want to make my marriage work, but life is so hectic with four kids under six, there isn't time. Besides, I don't know where to start."

Others joined our conversation, and a lively discussion followed. What are the characteristics of a healthy marriage? The group mentioned commitment, faith in God, good communication, romance, and common goals. But if we had to put it in a nutshell, we'd say, "A healthy marriage is one in which there is a willingness to find time to work on your relationship."

"Great," Kelly said. "But with four kids and a part-time job, do you think I can really find time to work on my marriage?"

"Yes," I (Dave) answered. "But you have to be intentional."

According to a poll of twelve thousand people, the number one cause of marriage failures is simply not working on the marriage. No one plans to be a divorce statistic, but life happens, relationships slip, marriages break up. But all the news isn't bad—the number one cause of divorce is preventable!

We took our own informal survey and asked

people why they didn't work on their marriage. And the overwhelming answer was "lack of time."

It takes time to grow a healthy marriage, and we continually have to look for moments to invest. We've been working on our marriage for over thirty-five years, and time and time again we still have to regroup, reprioritize, and free up moments for each other. And when we get too busy, God is faithful to remind us. In the midst of our business, we hear His whisper . . . *It's time to slow down, time to talk, to reconnect, to invest in your relationship.*

Stand at the crossroads and look; ask for the ancient paths, ask where the good way is, and walk in it, and you will find rest for your souls.

JEREMIAH 6:16

And when we experience His gentle nudge, we put on the breaks. It's the way to avoid trouble up ahead and to keep our relationship going in the right direction.

Quiet Whispers from God's Heart for Couples

The gentle breeze coming through the open window laden with geraniums was a welcomed guest on this late spring day as we lunched with our old friends. Rainer looked tenderly at Christa as he helped pull her sweater over her shoulders.

For the past fifteen years she had been in and out of hospitals interspersed with days, months, and years of no energy, poor health, and little hope of ever being well again. The doctor's puzzlement as to the diagnosis of her condition was a chronic frustration, as were their unanswered questions and prayers to God for healing and strength.

But today we were celebrating. At last, some of Christa's strength had returned, as evidenced by our lunch together at this lovely old farm restaurant. As we thanked God for the delicious food we also thanked him for Christa's improving health. Then we asked how they had survived the last fifteen years. Rainer answered, "We took life one day at a time."

Christa continued, "God has been so good to us. We've learned so much about His faithfulness. My illness has actually brought us closer together. We don't know what the future holds, but we have peace day by day as God whispers to us . . . *I will be with you in sickness and in health*. We know He holds the future and that He is watching over us."

No complaints. No bitterness. Fifteen years of struggles, yet no evidence of anger. Privately, we wondered how we would handle life if we were faced with similar difficulties.

We could never be brave and patient if there were only joy in the world.

HELEN KELLER

Later that afternoon, after we had said good-bye to our friends, we got in our car and headed back to our hotel deep in the Black Forest of Southern Germany. As we traversed the curving mountain roads we struggled with our own lingering questions. In the silence we found answers as God whispered to our hearts . . . *Don't fear the future. I will be with you—in sickness and in health.*

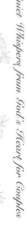

At last the children were in bed and asleep. We slipped quietly out the front door of our chalet. Time for *us*. Time for a short walk and a breath of fresh air.

How close the stars looked! The diamond-studded sky illuminated the snow-covered path.

Walking together in the snow was a great way to end a fun but exhausting day. We had spent the day teaching our youngest son how to manage the T-bar ski lift. And our two older sons still needed supervision. Ski vacations at this stage of family life were not that relaxing. But now was our time. A few minutes to be alone. To walk and talk in the snow . . . to refocus on us. With three small sons, focusing on our marriage was getting harder and harder to do.

We missed the carefree days when "fun" was an integral part of each day. Now we were "the parents" and too often "the serious parents" . . . the disciplinarians . . . the family policemen. We had come a long way from our carefree dating days.

As we walked in the snow, I (Claudia) asked Dave, "When you were a kid, did you ever make angels in the snow?"

Before he could answer, I just did it! I laid down in the pristine snow by the side of the road, moved my arms and legs up and down, and made an angel!

Dave broke into laughter and joined me. We made a whole platoon of snow angels. As we laughed at ourselves, we promised ourselves we would never completely grow up.

As if giving His seal of approval, our Heavenly Father seemed to whisper . . . *Take time to play, to be childlike, to enjoy the beautiful world I created for your pleasure! Don't take yourself so seriously.*

Snowflakes are one of nature's most fragile things, but just look at what they can do when they stick together.

VESTA M. KELLY

We looked at each other, and Dave threw the first snowball. That was one fight we both won.

Years later, we still remember that night of hugging, kissing, and playing in the snow. And we still remember God's whisper to never completely grow up—to take time to play and enjoy His wonderful creation called *life*.

Quiet Whispers from God's Heart for Couples

We sat across the table from Zoe as she answered our questions. Our assignment, as part of the International Year of the Family at the United Nations in Vienna, Austria, was to interview people from as many different nationalities as possible to discover the positive things that families were doing around the world.

Zoe was one of the most delightful people we talked to. She was from Brazil, married to a German. Two radically different cultures, yet their marriage seemed to work. We wanted to discover their secret, and as Zoe began to talk, we did:

Tossing The Wedding Bouquet
© Wooster Scott

"Hans and I are radically different. He's organized and likes structure. Without him I would be a mess. I'm the spontaneous one, and, I must admit, I'm a random person. My motto is 'Que sera sera'—whatever will be will be!

"When we were first married, we didn't get along that well. Our different cultural backgrounds complicated our relationship. For instance, Hans expected us to eat dinner at six each evening—just like clockwork! My desire was to have dinner when we were hungry and certainly not before eight or nine PM. I didn't want to get in a boring routine.

"Then we began to realize that God had created each of us unique. If we trusted Him, He could mold us together as one, with the best from each benefiting the other. Now our relationship is great. Our differences give texture to our marriage. Hans keeps us organized and focused, and I, well, I liven things up!"

The twinkle in Zoe's eyes validated her words. This very different cross-cultural marriage worked. The secret? In our hearts we knew . . . *Let your God-given differences enhance your relationship.* It's one secret smart couples know.

Accept one another, then, just as Christ accepted you, in order to bring praise to God.

ROMANS 15:7

Quiet Whispers from God's Heart for Couples

The year was 1972. The phone rang. I (Dave) answered it. On the other end was my director. Would I teach at an up-coming conference in West Virginia?

Actually, it wasn't "Would I be there?" it was "You will be there!" But there was a dilemma—Claudia was very pregnant with our third child, and the conference was to be in a remote mountain retreat center. There would be no quick way to get home

in case the baby came early or Claudia needed me.

I was perplexed. If I were truly spiritual, my director had insinuated, I would trust God with my family. The director needed me at the conference. I prayed and pleaded with God to change my director's mind . . . but He didn't. There was still no resolution —just a brick wall.

Finally, alone on my knees, I cried out to God, "If You aren't going to change him, then please show me what I'm suppose to do." Silently, I waited—and then in the quietness, I suddenly knew what I had to do. Almost in an audible whisper, God spoke to my heart . . . *Dave, there will be many other conferences in which you will teach, but only one opportunity to be present at the birth of your baby.*

Later that day I told Claudia, "I'm not going to the conference—even if I get fired."

We both felt God's peace, and I knew I had made the right decision. Especially when Jonathan was born a couple of weeks early—at the exact time I would have been away at that conference. And amazingly, the director accepted my decision. He didn't fire me, and I kept my job.

For me, that was one of those defining moments when I chose to make my marriage a priority. Since that time Claudia has never doubted that she and our children come first!

> *Call to me and I will answer you and tell you great and unsearchable things you do not know.*
>
> JEREMIAH 33:3

Quiet Whispers from God's Heart for Couples

3 5

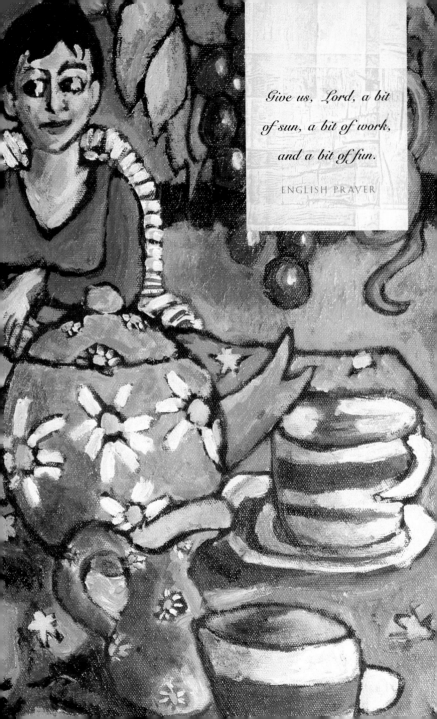

Give us, Lord, a bit
of sun, a bit of work,
and a bit of fun.

ENGLISH PRAYER

Totally exhausted, we sat in our car glaring at each other. "Why do we do this to ourselves?" I (Claudia) asked.

"I really don't know, but something has to give!" Dave answered.

We had just finished giving a program on dating. But we couldn't remember our last date. And on this evening there would be no "on-the-way-home-stop-off-for-coffee-date." We still had to race to FedEx to get off the corrected manuscript for a book we were writing on how to build a creative love life. Some lovers we were. On that evening we would have settled for a love moment—let alone a love life!

We had become so consumed with helping other couples that we were in danger of letting our own relationship slip. Of course we rationalized, "Helping others keeps us working on our own marriage." Yet on that evening as we headed for the FedEx office instead of each other's arms, we knew in our hearts we were wrong. Where were the boundaries between our work and our marriage?

Later as we drove home, we agreed to make some changes. At that moment we knew . . . *Our work will wait while we grab some time for our marriage, but our marriage won't wait until we finish our work.*

After our frantic FedEx experience, we knew we needed to make some changes. Together we looked at our upcoming schedule, got out our red pen, and used it on our calendar. Then we planned several days away just for us.

And now, even years later, when the boundary between work and marriage begins to get fuzzy, we declare a marriage evening. We leave the television off, let the voice mail get our calls, light a candle, put on soft music, and celebrate our marriage!

J ohn, a successful surgeon, had his life all mapped out—his practice, his golf, and his family. Sarah, a dedicated mother and community leader, seemed focused and settled in her life as well. Then one day Sarah asked John, "What do you really want out of life?"

She was totally unprepared for his answer, "Sarah, I want our marriage to be better!"

Looking at each other in shock, they began to talk about their relationship. Before long they realized . . . *We can have a better marriage if we want it.*

Together, they began a journey that would span more than a decade and would lead them to a deeper, more satisfying relationship. Their success is recorded in a letter written to us just before John retired. Let us share part of it with you:

Dear Dave and Claudia,

In thinking about our forty-one years of marriage, we asked ourselves what we'd learned and how we feel as we close this chapter of our life and begin our adventure into retirement. By far, the greatest discovery we've made was that we can change and *should* change! At first the thought of change was very threatening, but when we discovered we *could*, it became exciting.

We had to relearn how to listen to each other. . . . Becoming better listeners, being more honest, more careful, and more companionable, we learned much about ourselves and about each other. Also we developed more trust and reliance on each other as we learned how to work together.

The development of a really good marriage is not a natural process. It's an achievement.

DAVID AND VERA MACE

Finally, we feel we have reinvented our marriage relationship in a manner compatible with this stage of life. Now we look forward to the next chapter of our life together with great optimism and enthusiasm. . . .

Best of friends,
John and Sarah*

Like our friends, the McCrackens, all who are willing to choose to work at it can have a better marriage!

*(Adapted from *The Second Half of Marriage,* by David and Claudia Arp, Zondervan)

Quiet Whispers from God's Heart for Couples

Walking hand-in-hand through the silent woods, we paused to appreciate the beauty. With the backdrop of the towering Alps, the snow-laden evergreens reminded us of a favorite calendar on the wall in our home office. The majesty of God shouts from every mountain peak, but how easy it is for us to miss it back home when we get too busy.

So as an antidote to our own busyness and a celebration of making it through yet another year,

we are here at our favorite hideaway in Obendorf, a little village tucked away in the Austrian Alps. Here to relax, write, and reconnect with each other.

Here in the Alp's it's easy to feel God's presence—to

hear Him whisper . . . *Slow down and enjoy my creation. I am the One who formed the mountains, the trees. Each snowflake is an original design. I also created you. Take time to acknowledge Me and walk together on My path. It's the path of blessing.*

They will speak of the glorious splendor of your majesty, and I will mediate on your wonderful works.

PSALM 145:5

We pause and thank God for helping us through another year and for giving us this moment of peace and tranquility.

Let us encourage you, wherever you are, to pause and appreciate God's handiwork. You may not be able to see the Alps or walk through the snow, but you can turn off the television and appreciate the silence. Or stop for a moment to look at a sleeping baby, or watch a sunset or smell a flower.

Remember, God created it all. Let Him help you slow down. He's the One who stills the roaring of the sea and waves. He waters the land with rain and makes the crops grow. If God's power is so awesome in nature, can't we also trust Him with our lives and our marriages?

It's something to think about.

Room by room, we slowly walked through our family home one last time. Our words echoed off the empty walls as we randomly grabbed memories from two decades of family life. "Dave, do you remember when we first found this house and there was the ice-maker hookup we needed?" I (Claudia) asked.

We smiled at each other, remembering how years ago we had scraped together our pennies for the down payment and how that ice-maker hookup in some strange way had confirmed that this was to be our home!

"Yes," Dave replied. "And remember how huge this house felt when we moved here with our two preschoolers?"

Our children had grown up in this house. Now all three sons were gone, and the real-estate sign in our yard read, "Sold." We were saying goodbye to our wonderful family home that had too much yard and too much room for just the two of us. Reality hit. We were moving. Our life was changing.

We were actually entering a new stage of life: a time to downsize—a time to refocus. What lay ahead? With some apprehension, we closed the door of our family home for the last time, walked down the sidewalk, and got into the car.

We knew God would go with us into the unknown future. With His help we could surmount the empty-nest challenges to share our dreams, to make fresh commitments, and to work toward a more satisfying union. Together we would embrace this new season of life.

As we backed out of our driveway for the last time, our hearts were comforted with an unspoken whisper—*Change is as certain as the seasons. Embrace it! I will go with you.*

Pulling into the traffic, we turned at the next corner. Our future awaited us, and with God's assurance, we could face it with optimistic enthusiasm. The rest just might be the best!

Life has taught us that love does not consist in gazing at each other but in looking outward together in the same direction.

ANTOINE DE SAINT-EXUPERY

P erhaps you have heard the story of Robertson and Muriel McQuilkin. He served as president of a Christian college, and she, also very gifted and articulate, worked in media.

Then the unthinkable happened. Muriel's memory began to fade and became increasingly worse. The day Muriel was diagnosed with Alzheimer's their lives changed forever. Their forty-two-year marriage would never be the same. But what did not change was Robertson's commitment to love his wife in sickness and in health. He was still several years from retirement, and as the disease progressed, friends encouraged him to put Muriel in an institution. He simply would not consider it and told his friends that in an institution no one would love her the way he did.

When we heard this story, we looked at each other and wondered how we would respond in a similar situation. Would God give us the grace to remain faithful? Could we bear the pain of watching the other slowly decline? Could we deal with the mood and personality changes that accompany Alzheimer's? How would we cope?

Then in the middle of our fears and our questions, God whispered to our hearts . . . *My grace is sufficient for you. Whatever you may walk through,*

I will go with you. My faithfulness endures forever.

God forbid that we—or you —would ever have to walk the same path as Robertson and Muriel McQuilkin. But if the unthinkable happens, we can be assured that our Heavenly Father will give us the grace to remain faithful to each other. While God may not lead you to quit your job, as He led Robertson McQuilkin,

For great is his love toward us, and the faithfulness of the Lord endures forever.

PSALM 117:2

you can know that He will go before you and show you the way you should go.

Remember, His grace is sufficient and His faithfulness endures forever.

Quiet Whispers from God's Heart for Couples

The rows of young corn plants resembled a military marching band with tassels swaying in the late afternoon breeze. Rain was in the forecast. As I (Claudia) hurried to finish weeding, I could picture our family sitting around the table eating corn on the cob that was dripping with melted butter. Yum!

My vegetable garden was my pride and joy. For the previous five years we had lived in an apartment in Vienna, Austria. So to have a yard again was great. But the real treat was having my very own vegetable garden, and soon corn from it would be on our table!

Then the storm came. High winds. Thunder. Lightening. Inches of rain. Early the next morning we surveyed the damage. The rows of corn were now in disarray. It looked like a herd of cattle had trampled through our garden!

"Dave, it's just not fair!" I cried. "I worked so hard, and now my corn is ruined."

"Not to worry." Dave said consolingly. "I'll get some string and stakes and we'll tie the plants back up."

After hours of hard work, we surveyed our garden. Each corn plant was now a prisoner securely tied to a stake. About that time our neighbor Carol, who was a seasoned gardener, came over, looked at our tied-up corn plants, and burst into laughter. "Why on earth did you do that?" she asked. "Don't you know that when the sun comes out, the warmth of its rays will cause the corn to straighten up?"

The garden is the place were we discover that faith is a work of art.

HARRIET CROSBY

We looked at each other. Muddy, tired, and exhausted, we realize we had worked in vain to do what nature would do on its own. We needed to work *with* nature—not help nature out. We really couldn't control the weather, and we couldn't control our corn plants. But God, who created nature, had it all under control.

How foolish we felt. Later, when we reflected on our gardening experiences, we realized that it's just as foolish to try to manipulate each other. To get all tied up trying to fix and control everything about each other. Sometimes we need to let God's sunlight do the correcting. Yes, that was it. At that point we understood . . . *Our Heavenly Father is the Gardener of our marriage. He sends the rain and the wind, and He sends the sunshine. His healing power will make our relationship grow.*

So what happened to our garden that year? In our attempt to save our corn, we unintentionally

Quiet Whispers from God's Heart for Couples

packed the soil and
disturbed the plants.
We had some corn, but
the plants never quite
recovered. The next year
we saved our string and
stakes and let the sun
take care of things.

We also tried to be
more sensitive with each
other. Like our garden,
our marriage requires a
lot of work and attention.
We need to shower each
other with support and
encouragement. And
when our marriage gets
hit by the storms of life,
we look to God and ask
Him to send warm rays
of healing. We want to
keep cultivating our
"marriage garden" so that
in the future we can reap
the fruit of a healthy
relationship.

*Keep my commands
and you will live.*

PROVERBS 7

CHOOSE FAITHFULNESS

A glance across the room. Eyes lock. Chemistry. Unwanted chemistry—but there just the same. Frank thought of Lydia—his love, his wife for over a decade. What was happening?

And then deep within his heart, he heard God's silent whisper . . . *Flee! Go! You have a choice. Choose fidelity. Choose faithfulness. It's the path of blessing!*

Without looking back, Frank walked out of the room, grateful to God for His gentle nudge. On this day Frank chose the narrow road of faithfulness and fidelity.

In today's world, temptation seems to lurk behind every corner. Have you felt it—a sudden attraction to someone other than your spouse? A look, a random touch, a listening ear on the day your marriage partner seems deaf? If you haven't, chances are you will. So let us encourage you. When it happens, listen for the gentle whisper, *Flee! Go! Choose faithfulness. It's the path of blessing.*

You'll be glad you did.

O n a late spring day, we slipped away for a cup of cappuccino at a little sidewalk café on the edge of a lake. The water glistened in the afternoon sun. As we sipped our coffee, we watched the ducks splashing in the water. All was calm and peaceful.

Nearby, we observed a young family, complete with a baby in a stroller, also enjoying the ducks. Suddenly, the baby threw her pacifier to the ducks, and an amazing thing happened. The ducks began to fight over the pacifier. First the mama and the papa duck fought for it. The winner would swim around, pacifier in its beak, until the other duck would swipe it away. Then the little ducklings got into the act. Each was determined to win the pacifier, which, of course, was useless to them. We laughed at how ridiculous the ducks looked with that pacifier in their beaks.

Who lives content with little possesses everything.

NICOLAS BOILEAU-DESPREAUX

Then we began to think . . . *Aren't we sometimes like those ducks? Don't we struggle to grasp things we don't need? How much time do we spend chasing useless things we think will pacify us?*

It's a fallacy to believe that "the one with the most toys wins." Things never have and never will satisfy. Without realizing it, sometimes we are as silly as those ducks. We asked ourselves, *What fruitless goals are we chasing? What are the "pacifiers" of our lives? Are our priorities out of order because of our desire to have things that don't really satisfy?* We realized it was time to reevaluate our lifestyle—time to consolidate and simplify.

We left the sidewalk café with a new zest to invest in the important things of life and in the future. The ducks can have the pacifiers!

Alone at last, Steve and Jan looked at each other across the candle-lit table. The old Italian restaurant was a perfect setting in which to celebrate their twelfth wedding anniversary.

"I wasn't sure we were ever going to get here," Jan said. Then she rattled off how she had coordinated meals, piano lessons, homework, ballet, and had even found another dad to sub for Steve at soccer practice.

"Now that you brought up soccer," Steve said, "I'm concerned about the lack of parental support for the team."

Jan then mentioned the problem with Hannah's kindergarten teacher—and Joey simply couldn't start nursery school until he was potty-trained.

Over dinner the conversation moved from the kids to their budget. As usual, money was tight. "As a matter of fact," Jan said, "We should head home and relieve the babysitter."

At home, after putting Joey to bed, Jan and Steve snuggled on the couch to watch a video. But after a few minutes, both fell sound asleep. Some anniversary.

Then next morning, Jan and Steve rehashed the night before. Even after overcoming mountains of obstacles to celebrate their anniversary, they had spent most of the evening focusing on the kids, the finances—everything but their relationship.

Time is a very precious gift of God; so precious that it's only given to us moment by moment.

AMELIA BARR

"We used to be best friends, soul mates, lovers," Jan said. "Now it's more like we're running a business—a family business. We keep saying things will change, but nothing does."

"There's always a crisis—at work or at home. We just seem to run out of energy and time before we get to *us*." Steve added.

Discouraged, they looked at each other. And then they realized that, ultimately, it was up to them to make a change. In the silence, the whisper came . . . *It's never too early or too late to make changes! Today, you can choose to make your marriage a priority.*

That morning Steve and Jan made the choice. They agreed to try a thirty-one-day experiment. For the next month they would carve out ten minutes a day just to focus on each other. Whether early in the morning before the kids woke up, or in the evening after the kids were in bed, they agreed to spend ten minutes together and acknowledge it as their

The way to love anything is to realize that it might be lost.

G. K. CHESTERTON

"couple time."

During those thirty-one days, they faithfully claimed their couple time. Even when they were too tired to talk, they invested ten minutes simply sitting close and holding each other. Did it make a difference?

"Yes," Steve told us. "It was just a little step—just ten minutes a day—but we proved that little steps, if taken in good faith, can change everything."

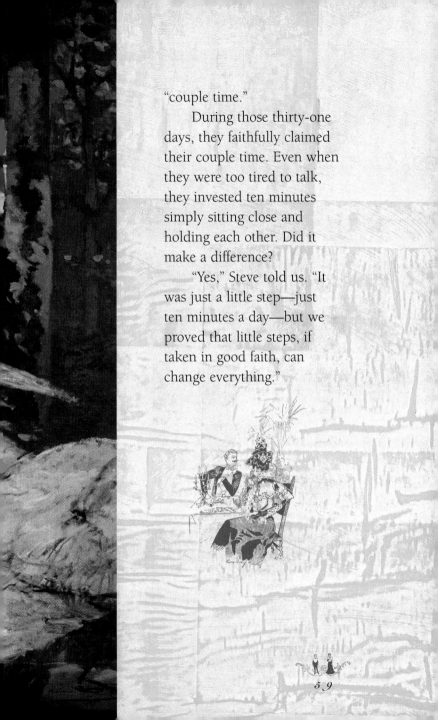

T ime. What is it? Sixty seconds make a minute, minutes turn into hours, and hours into days. Time zips by almost unnoticed. Then something happens and time seems to stand still. Life is never the same again.

It was one of those phone calls you dread. Lillian, Dave's mom, had suffered a stroke. In the next few weeks as she lingered between life and death, time stopped long enough for us to reflect on this remarkable woman and the seasons of her life and marriage.

Dave's parents were married for fifty-five years. As we reflected on their years together, we thought about our own marriage and a soft whisper challenged us . . . *Are you being good stewards of the time you still have together? How are you investing your marriage moments?*

Each season of marriage comes with different stress points and challenges. The casual discovery days of the first months and years accelerate into the hectic parenting years and on into the empty nest and the retirement season of life. The years quickly race by.

As we considered my parents' fifty-five years of marriage, I (Dave) remembered that when I was a young boy, my parents from time to time would go off alone together. As a teenager, I'd catch them hugging and kissing on the balcony. I remembered how as empty nesters, they were each other's best friends. Throughout the seasons of their marriage, they took time to love each other.

Do not be afraid, for I am with you,

GENESIS 26:24

Now Lillian is gone. We realize anew that our marriage is time bound and someday we too will be parted by death. We ask ourselves, *Are we being good stewards of the time we do have?*

The Time Is Now

If you are ever going to love me,
Love me now, while I can know
The sweet and tender feelings
Which from true affection flow.
Love me now
While I am living.
Do not wait until I'm gone
And then have it chiseled in marble,
Sweet words on ice-cold stone.
If you have tender thoughts of me,
Please tell me now.

ANONYMOUS

Jeanie smiled at her husband, Dave. "From the beginning of our marriage, we've had fun together. Even when the children came along, we still managed to find time for each other."

"Not as much time as before the kids, but we always found some time." Dave added. "And that didn't end when we entered the empty nest. We simply filled our nest with bunnies!"

When we visited in their home, sure enough, rabbits were everywhere! They even have four stuffed bunnies who travel with them. But their fun relationship is about more than bunnies. That's just the beginning.

Jeanie told us. "For years we've had pet names for each other, and not just two or three. We have hundreds!"

"What's your favorite?" I (Claudia) asked.

She answered with a smile, "Lover Bunny."

They also have special kisses. They send each other love letters. At airports they fake good-bye kisses and then get on the plane together. And at the grocery checkout counters, Dave often asks Jeanie to marry him all over again.

Their lightheartedness influences other areas in their relationship—even areas of conflict. Years ago they came up with the ten-minute silence rule. At any time, either can call for ten minutes of silence. If the nonverbal is a problem, they also have an out-of-sight-for-ten-minutes rule. This helps them calm down and get things back in perspective.

What has kept this couple's fifty-plus-year marriage happy and delightful? In our hearts we knew their secret . . . and then we heard a confirming whisper . . . *Fun and laughter are keys to a great marriage. Couples who play together, stay together!*

And Dave and Jeanie are the living proof!

If a man insisted always on being serious, and never allowed himself a bit of fun and relaxation, he would go mad or become unstable without knowing it.

HERODOTUS,
THE HISTORY OF
HERODOTUS, BOOK II

The illuminated seat-belt sign reinforced what I (Claudia) already knew—we were flying through turbulence. I checked the security of my seat belt. When the weather is sunny and the winds are calm, I like to fly. But on days like this one, I'd rather have my feet on the ground.

And how was Dave handling all this turbulence? Looking over at him, I was simply amazed! He was asleep. In the middle of this rough flight, he was actually sleeping! I desperately wanted to wake him up. What if it got worse? What if we hit wind shear?

As I tried unsuccessfully to relax, I began to think about how flying in planes is similar to building a marriage. Over the thirty-five-plus years of our marriage, we've lived through turbulent times. Every marriage experiences turbulence. Of course, you want to avoid severe and extreme turbulence if at all possible. And while some marital turbulence can be avoided, at times you simply must fly through it. Unfortunately when some couples experience problems, their marriages crash and burn. We've dedicated our lives to helping couples avoid marital disasters. So what could I learn from this mental exercise?

About that time the pilot came on the loud-speaker and said, "As you are aware we are experiencing turbulence. For the next few minutes it will continue to be bumpy, since we are flying right on top of the clouds." *Oh*, I thought. *On top of the clouds!* I began to relax a little bit now that I knew to expect a few more bumps. And with each bump, I tried to picture our plane skipping on the top of the clouds.

You will keep in perfect peace him whose mind is steadfast, because he trusts in you.

ISAIAH 26:3 (NIV)

Suddenly I understood, *It's possible to handle your fears of flying in bumpy weather or even turbulent times in a marriage if you know they are coming and if you stay on top of them!*

The key is to stay on top of them! Later, when Dave woke up (refreshed and unconcerned), I told him about the turbulence he missed and the pilot's comments and my analogy. Our conclusion? The only way to avoid turbulence in marriage is to stay on the ground and go nowhere. And there are those static boring marriages that do. But for couples who realize a little conflict is a given and who want to fly through it, their love for each other can grow. As our plane finely landed, we agreed we wanted to continue to grow through our own turbulent times. And from now on, when I'm faced with a rough flight I'll try to stay on top of the bumps!

Quiet Whispers from God's Heart for Couples

The year was 1961. We were desperately in love. . . young love, true love, filled with deep emotion. I (Claudia) was a freshman at Maryville College on the edge of the Great Smokey Mountains. I (Dave) was in my second year at Georgia Tech in Atlanta, Georgia. Two hundred miles apart! But we remember one time when Dave drove up for the weekend. Time for just the two of us! Time to be together.

Slipping away from the college campus, we drove to Cades Cove in the heart of the Smokies. And on that day we visited the past—others' past. Cades Cove, untouched by "American progress," is a tribute to the first families who settled there so many years ago. We imagined the young couples, in love and struggling for survival in the beautiful but isolated valley. We stood together in the Primitive Baptist church and talked about how someday, we would speak our marriage vows in the little Methodist church in Ellijay, Georgia, where Claudia grew up.

Almost four decades later, we revisited Cades Cove. We went back to the Primitive Baptist Church and once again remembered those lovers who went before us. We remembered our own wedding day in Watkins Memorial Methodist Church, December 28, 1962. We reminisced about all of our sons' weddings including the one that took place in Austria, where we lived during much of our children's growing-up years.

Each happiness of yesterday is a memory for tomorrow.

GEORGE WEBSTER DOUGLAS

Joel's words still echoed in our memory, "Mom, Dad, I want to go back to my past to begin my future." And so the Arp clan returned to our past to launch our son into his future.

As we revisited our memories we felt profoundly thankful for the heritage that was ours—for almost four decades of loving each other, and for three sons, all married and in loving relationships. But what did the future hold for our grandchildren? Would they ever experience the quietness and peacefulness of Cades Cove? Our world has become more complicated. Life is anything but primitive and peaceful. How would they fare? And in the middle of our memories and fears for the future, God whispered to our hearts, *Never forget your past, let it enrich your present, but you must trust Me for the future. I am the same, yesterday, today, and forever.*

And then we began to realize that the future— yet to be written—is in God's hands. Our children, grandchildren, and generations to come, will have their own unique love stories to write. But the greatest love story of all—God's love for us—will be the same yesterday, today, and forever.

Quiet Whispers from God's Heart for Couples

Thank goodness, this day is almost over," Paul said to his wife, Lucy. Several weeks ago Paul's mother, after a lengthy illness, had passed on from this world to the next. Today's daunting task—clearing out her condo and going through her personal things—left them both exhausted and emotionally drained.

Now one more load to the dumpster. Throughout the day, they had sorted through her stuff—boxes and boxes of letters, newspaper clippings, old magazines, and pictures of so many unknown people. Memorabilia others didn't want or care about. Junk that must have been precious to Paul's mother. As Paul threw away the last garbage bags, he stared at the dumpster and thought, "My Mom's life is in that dumpster."

Then it hit him—*one day that may be my stuff! What heritage am I leaving to my loved ones—a dumpster of stuff or a legacy of love and faith?*

Suddenly, Paul realized the choice was his. We also have choices to make. Os Guinness in *The Call* writes, "The trouble is that, as modern people, we have too much to live with and too little to live for. . . . Most of us, in the midst of material plenty, . . . have spiritual poverty. . . . Answering the call of our Creator is 'the ultimate why' for living, the highest source of purpose in human existence."

Have you answered God's call? What is God's calling for your marriage? Do you need to invest in more stuff? Probably not. Perhaps what you really need to invest in is more time. Time to declutter your lives; time to renew your love with long walks and talks. Precious moments invested in your marriage and family today will never end up in a dumpster tomorrow.

May your deeds be shown to your servants, your splendor to their children.

PSALM 90:16 (NIV)

d'après Renoir
Raoul Dufy

I will surely bless you and make your descendants as numerous as the stars in the sky and as the sand on the seashore.

GENESIS 22:24

The plane touched down. We were on foreign soil. Switzerland. Our three small sons in tow, we deplaned. The year was 1973, and it was official —we were foreign missionaries. Scared foreign missionaries.

John, a fellow worker, met our flight and drove us into the city to a small three-room apartment over a store. As we looked around our drab setting we observed the basics: beds, a stove and refrigerator, four chairs and a table.

"Take your time getting settled." And with that John was gone. The one link to our own culture drove down the street and disappeared into the distance.

We were alone. Alone with bare windows, street noise, a language we couldn't understand, no welcoming basket of fruit, no milk, no bread.

We looked at each other. Claudia cried. I (Dave) had no idea what to do. Jonathan, our fifteen-month-old, was just beginning to toddle, and he kept stubbing his toe on the threshold of the doors, each time falling down and crying—over and over again. Joel, our four-year-old, complained, "I'm hungry. I want something to eat!" Jarrett, our six-year-old, said, "I miss my friends. I miss my room. I want to go home!"

Here we were, in a foreign country to help others, yet we were so needy ourselves! Our mission at this point was survival. Claudia ventured to the store below our apartment. Somewhat successful, she came home with bread, milk, and bologna.

Tired, exhausted, discouraged. We finally got the boys to sleep. Sitting at the table, listening to the drizzling rain and the noisy street traffic, we looked at each other and cried to God for help. "God, did we misunderstand? Did we make a mistake? Why are we here?"

As we held each other, God met us at our time of greatest need, *You are here because I called you! Together you are here to serve me. I am faithful. I will do it. I will accomplish my will. I will never leave you helpless. Put your trust in me!*

Tears still flowed. Questions and uncertainty remained. But our Heavenly Father, who held the answers, comforted us. We could trust Him. Whatever trials, whatever adverse circumstances we might face, we could be confident that God is God and that He would be our God in this foreign and strange land. We turned off the light and went to sleep. Tomorrow was another day. Tomorrow was the future. God would walk through it with us.

The logs in the open fireplace crackled a warm welcome to the guests who had assembled to celebrate the union of Marcy and Steven. Outside the snow continued to fall. The ambience of the old hunting lodge on this cold winter day made a wonderful setting for a wedding reception.

The small intimate ceremony, completed just a few minutes ago, reaffirmed that God is the One who created the holy state of matrimony. Vows spoken. Two lives joined as one. Two hearts fused

together in love. Now the celebration.

In the background a classical guitar and flute filled the room with romantic chords. Each instrument complemented the other. Wonderful two-part harmony! And then God seemed to whisper . . . *Marriage is a two-part harmony—you both have your own notes to play. Play them in such a way that you complement and harmonize with one another.*

What a beautiful picture of a marriage! Two lives harmonizing together to create a new entity—a marriage. But too often we want to play our own song without harmonizing with the other. Or we want to be our own voice rather than blending together as one. Yet in a duet each seeks to enhance the other so that together the music is more beautiful than it would have been with just one playing or singing alone.

In a harmonious marriage there is no room for competition or tooting our own horn. Competing is the opposite of harmonizing. If we're playing in harmony, it means we mutually respect each other and our unique gifts. It really is as if we are two different musical instruments playing different parts. With God's grace we can continue to make beautiful music together!

Do nothing out of selfish ambition or vain conceit, but in humility consider others better than yourselves."

PHILIPPIANS 2:3 (NIV)

We'll never forget that crisp, clear, fall day when we dropped our last son off at college. Jonathan looked so young and vulnerable, but we knew he was ready to face the challenges college life would present him. We weren't so sure about ourselves! Slowly we got in our car, backed out of the freshman dormitory parking lot, waved our last good-byes, and began the ten-hour trip home to Knoxville, Tennessee.

As the miles slipped by, an unfamiliar cloud of silence descended. Usually chatty, I (Claudia) was pensive . . . reflective . . . almost disoriented as we entered the uncharted waters of the empty nest. The first dilemma—Dave wanted to take the slow road home. After all, what was the big hurry?

I wanted to get home ASAP and Lysol the house! But then what? Neither of us knew. So much of our lives had been consumed with parenting our three sons—actually our marriage and family ministry grew out of our love for family—but now what?

Working as marriage educators, we knew the divorce rate soars in the empty-nest years and that every marriage—including our own—was vulnerable. Each spouse faces unique challenges. Women must deal with menopause and the signs of aging in a youth-oriented world; plus they lose their major job as resident mom. On the other hand, at this stage men often reach the peak of prestige. Their egos soar. I still remember how a few gray hairs made Dave even more attractive—and I wasn't the only woman who noticed. Definitely not a confidence builder!

So that fall, as the leaves turned, we both turned to the One who created marriage. Looking at familiar verses through the lens of the empty nest, God filled our hearts with a new zest and excitement for investing in our own marriage and honoring Him with the second half of our lives. Our marriage verses, Ecclesiastes 4:9–12, took on new meaning as God whispered to us . . . *Two are better than one . . . and now you are two again. So embrace the empty nest.*

As we attempted to reinvent our marriage for the second half, we discovered that while we lacked energy and stamina, God had blessed us with patience, experience, and balance. Together we worked to create a more partner-focused rather than child-focused marriage.

Now almost a decade into our empty-nest journey, we're still learning to adapt to the changing landscape, but each fall as we watch the leaves paint the countryside with unrivaled beauty, we're reminded of God's provision for every stage of life. And Robert Browning's words are etched in our hearts, *"Grow old along with me, the best is yet to be."* With God's help, it will be!

The dinner was exquisite, the atmosphere, romantic. The setting? A thirteenth-century castle, set high on a hill overlooking the medieval town of Esslingen, Germany. Sharing this special evening were our friends, Dorothea and Dankfried. Between us, we had logged over fifty-three years of marriage. Over dinner we talked about what marriage must have been like in the thirteenth century. Then the conversation turned to the state of marriage today.

"What's happening to

marriages here in Germany is disturbing," Dankfried told us. "Many couples—even before they say *I do*, lack the commitment to love each other for a lifetime!"

"In some of the more modern marriage liturgies," Dorothea added, "couples commit themselves to stay together until love dies not until death parts."

A chilling thought—as chilling as the stone walls of that old castle! What causes love to die? What causes love to live? And then it hit us . . . *For love to last, you must give up other options! Exercising your commitment strengthens your love muscles.*

There, surrounded by history, we renewed our commitment to nurture our love, to stick together through thick and thin, to keep on accepting and forgiving each other. And as we vowed in our own wedding liturgy so many years ago, to forsake all others!

Quiet Whispers from God's Heart for Couples

Five of the six couples I'm presently working with," a counselor told us, "are facing a medical crisis and can expect to lose their spouse in the next six months."

We were speaking at a conference on how to build a successful long-term marriage and this counselor challenged us. "For these couples "long-term" is a cruel joke.

Her comments made us stop and think. "If one of us had only six months to live, what changes would we make?"

A few days later we heard another story and decided not to wait until we just have six months to change our perspective. Bob and Betty had been married for forty-two years and most of those years Bob had pastored a small country church. They loved having their grandchildren visit and looked forward to their retirement years. Bob was planning to retire at the first of the year.

At first he hardly noticed the headaches, but finally he decided to go to his doctor. He couldn't believe the words he was hearing! "Bob, you probably have six months—perhaps eight."

Suddenly, everything changed for Bob and Betty. What was so important last week, wasn't now.

Heartbroken, they began to talk about their immediate future. Then Betty did something out-of-character for both of them.

They had always lived very modestly. However, recently Betty had received a small inheritance. What she did with her windfall was both unexpected and extravagant. She bought Bob a red Mercedes convertible! Every day she took Bob for an afternoon drive in the new red Mercedes. And when the weather was nice, she put the top down. With the wind in their faces, they chose to focus on the present and to leave their fears and worry at home. Betty chose to be extravagant with her love and to celebrate their marriage for as many days as God chose to give them.

When we heard their story, our hearts were touched, and we asked ourselves, *Are we as extravagant with our love?* And then we knew in our hearts, *You can be! Start now. Celebrate your marriage. Love each other with abandon!*

While no red Mercedes convertible is in our foreseeable future, we are trying to be more extravagant with our time and energy. We're being more liberal with our compliments. We're planning more dates. Hugging each other a little tighter. Kissing a little longer.

How about you? Are you extravagant with your love? It's something to think about.

Life is short, and we have never too much time for gladdening the hearts of those who are traveling the dark journey with us. Oh, be swift to love, make haste to be kind!

HENRI FREDERIC AMIEL

We sat in city traffic anxious to get home. The next day we were leaving for a series of conferences, and once again we were in the panic mode—too much to do and too little time!

"Why do we always overcommit ourselves?" I (Dave) asked.

Staring at the brake lights of the car in front of us, Claudia replied. "I don't know, but I do know something has got to give. We simply can't keep us this pace!"

About that time on a voice on our car radio asked, "Are you experiencing fast-lane stress in your marriage?"

We looked at each other and said in unison, "Yes!"

The radio spot that day seemed customized for us. We continued to listen. "If you're experiencing fast-lane stress, here's a tip for you. Sit down and make a list of all the things you need to do. Then prioritize your list. Put the most important thing first and start there. You may not get everything done in one day, but you will go to bed at night knowing you have invested your time in doing the most important. Think about this—life is too precious to hurry through it."

The last seven words changed our day. It was as if God had spoken directly to us in a quiet whisper . . . *Dave, Claudia, your lives are too precious to hurry through them! Slow down and trust me!*

As the traffic began to move once again, we knew what we needed to do. We drove straight home and over two cups of coffee we made our list and prioritized it. Then we divided the most important things that needed to be done before we left the next day.

The results? We didn't get everything checked off our lists, but we stopped hurrying. On that day we realized just how precious life is and how much we valued our marriage. And we vowed that in the future, when we get in a hurry, we will remind each other to slow down. By the way, what we heard that day on our car radio was our own two-minute program, *The Family Workshop*, and the couple we were listening to was ourselves!

Sometimes even we take our own good advice!

We may run, walk, stumble, drive, or fly, but let us never lose sight of the reason for the journey, or miss a chance to see a rainbow on the way.

GLORIA GAITHER

S itting with our friend Vera on the screened porch at her home in Black Mountain, North Carolina, we commented on how much she and David must have enjoyed rocking on their porch and looking at the magnificent Blue Ridge Mountains.

Vera chuckled. "Eventually, we did, but we almost didn't have a screened porch! You see," she continued, "we couldn't agree on how to go about it. The problem was that David's favorite tree was right here in the middle of where the porch needed to go. I wanted to cut it down. David didn't. I still remember the conversation:

'Vera,' David said, 'how could we even consider cutting down this tree? It's older than we are!'

'If we want to build our porch,' I replied to David, 'the tree will have to go. There simply isn't another spot for it.'

"Back and forth we went, each desperately wanting our own way. Finally David capitulated. Giving me a gift of love, he said, 'We shall cut down the tree. You shall have your screened porch!' "

"Did David ever regret giving in to you?" Claudia asked.

Vera laughed, "No, not at all! You see, when the tree came down, we discovered it was hollow. The inside had rotted away. It was good riddance! And if David had insisted on keeping the tree, in its weakened state a wind storm could have blown it over on our home."

What do we live for, if it is not to make life less difficult for each other?

GEORGE ELIOT

Then we realized how that tree is like marriage . . . *selfishness leads to decay; deferring to the other leads to blessing.*

Just as Vera and David's tree appeared to be fine, our marriage may look great on the outside, but if we selfishly demand our own way, our marriage will decay on the inside. Over time, our relationship can become hollow, weak, and rotten. But when we defer to each other, we strengthen our relationship.

Years later, when we remember Vera's tree story, we are challenged to work on our marriage—to cut down our own trees of selfishness and to defer to the other. Then we can help other couples build better marriages, and hopefully in the sunset of our lives, we will also enjoy rocking on our own screened porch.

Sam and Emily stared at each other over their cups of coffee. Suddenly they realized how far apart they had drifted. They didn't even agree about their recent move to the West Coast. Emily missed her close-knit family in New England. Sam just didn't understand.

"Why can't you be more supportive?" he asked. This was his opportunity to move into the leadership of a national Christian ministry. After all, this wasn't just a job, it was a calling.

Emily reminded him. "But, it's not *my* calling! I miss my home, my friends. I feel so alone." The stress of moving a family of five all the way across the United States had taken its toll. Tears welled up in Emily's eyes.

Sam stared in helpless silence. They knew each other so well—and yet they were strangers.

"How have we gotten so disconnected?" Sam asked.

"I don't know." Emily answered. "But I do know that deep down we love each other. Surely we can work things out."

The one thing they did agree on that morning was that they wanted to start over—to begin again. But how? In Maine they had always been so close—

especially when they took time to pray together. Now that seemed impossible. Or was it? Did God understand? Could their Heavenly Father help them bridge the chasm that separated them?

Sheepishly Sam said, "We could try praying together. That used to help."

Emily, wiping away the tears, looked at Sam with a faint glimmer of hope. "We can give it a try. We certainly don't have anything to loose."

Sam reached for Emily's hand and began to pray. "God, if you are here, we need your help."

Do not worry about anything; instead pray about everything; tell God your needs and don't forget to thank him for his answers.

PHILIPPIANS 4:6 (TLB)

And then it was as if God whispered to them, *I am always here. You are the ones who moved. Not just away from Maine, but also away from Me. I am always ready to listen, to hear your prayers and to meet the deepest needs of your hearts. Don't hold back. Call unto me and I will restore you and renew your marriage.*

Together they poured out their fears and concerns to each other and to God. And in the silence, they connected at a deeper level. Heart to heart they renewed their commitment to each other and to God.

In the coming weeks, they would live out their

Quiet Whispers from God's Heart for Couples

commitment in practical ways—like listening to each other when one would have preferred going to sleep, putting the other first through little daily acts of kindness, and mounting a concerted effort to replace a negative thought with a positive one. And in those times they disagreed or began to experience self-pity, they would stop and listen for God's voice. And as they prayed together they would again discover God's refreshment for the soul of their marriage.

H e held her close as she gently sobbed. Unspoken words. She squeezed his hand—each seeking to comfort the other.

Such highs. Such lows. The excitement, "We're going to be parents!" Unspeakable joy. A glorious future. A child's laugh to be. Awe. The continuation of the cycle of life!

Then the unfathomable word—"miscarriage"— the death of a baby yet to be born. Doctors, hospitals, tears, the reality of what would never be. They held each other, partners in pain. Then in the midst of their suffering God whispered to their hearts . . . *You do not need to understand the past or the present to trust Me with the future. I know the plans I have for you—they are for your good so that you may have hope.*

Days turned into weeks. Weeks turned into months. God's promise became the salve that soothed the pain. Time passes. Years go by. The scene changes. God's plan unfolds.

Once again they rush to the hospital. Breathe! Breathe! Relax! Breathe! Push! Push! A child is born. A new life is given. A new future created. Hope realized is a tree of life. The couple rejoices. A baby gasps for air and cries. The cycle of life continues.

Hope deferred makes
the heart sick,
But a longing
fulfilled is a
tree of life.

PROVERBS 13:12 (NIV)

W hat should have been a lovely drive through the Austrian Alps was not. Instead we could see nothing—just miles and miles of fog. We had looked forward to driving back to Zurich, Switzerland, to catch our ten-hour flight home, but now the fog.

Then, near Innsbruck, the dreary sky hiding the Alps gradually became brighter and brighter, and in one magic moment the fog at the very top of the Alps broke. We could finally see the tips of the Alps. But the next moment they disappeared, as if playing hide and seek with us. Fog. Alps. Fog. Alps.

How breathtaking it was when the fog lifted and we could see the majesty of the Alps! How disappointing when the thick fog reappeared! But isn't this how life is sometimes? Or even, on occasions, our marriage? At times we see so clearly the beauty all around us—and at other times we only see the fog. Yet, like the Alps in the fog, the beauty is always there whether we can see it or not!

As we continued to drive toward Innsbruck, we talked about times we have felt close to God and other times when we felt only distance. And then God seemed to speak to our hearts . . . *Like the Alps, I am there even when you don't see me! Trust Me in the foggy times as well as the sunny times in your life and in your marriage.*

Oh, if we could only remember this lesson—especially when we're in a fog of discouragement. God is there in the foggy times just as He is there when all is sunny in our lives. We need to trust Him both times.

And then as we approached the outskirts of Innsbruck, the sun suddenly broke through. We were surrounded by God's majesty—

As the mountains surround Jerusalem, so the Lord surrounds his people both now and forever.

PSALM 125:2

360 degrees of magnificent stately Alps! We promised each other we would remember this day and when fog reappeared we would remind each other that in the midst of the darkness and dullness, God is still there—even when we don't feel His presence! His love and protection—much more majestic than the Alps—always surrounds us!

When we moved to our condo, we wanted to add a few trees as a privacy buffer. Our friend Radio agreed to help plant them for us. Since we were leaving for a conference, we took Radio's suggestion and left our new trees just where we wanted them planted.

Soon after we left, a huge storm raced through Knoxville. When Radio came to plant the new trees, they were somewhat in the area we wanted them planted even though the storm had rearranged them. That part worked out fine, but our tropical ficus tree had blown off the deck and Radio planted it too!

The prognosis for a tropical plant surviving a Knoxville winter is not good. So after several more weeks of glorying in the fall sunshine—and, we might add, thriving—we replanted the ficus tree in a larger pot. After giving it a few days to acclimatize, we moved it inside for the winter. The results? It's never been so healthy! Being uprooted and replanted was like a shot of vitamins for that little tree.

As we laughed about the ficus tree, we thought about our marriage. Could our ficus story represent what God so often does with us? Just when we start to get complacent, He sends something—even storms—into our lives to stir us up. He replants us!

And then like a soft whisper God spoke to our hearts . . . *Change is inevitable, growth is optional. The changes and even the storms of life can cause you to grow closer together. Don't settle for a root-bound marriage!*

At that moment we realized that even mistakes can shake us out of complacency and jump–start growth. Our ficus tree is a living example.

And what did we do with the hole vacated by our ficus tree? We

Courageous risks are life giving, they help you grow, make you brave and better than you think you are.

MARIE CURIE

found a more appropriate holly tree to take its place, and each time we see it, it reminds us of our ficus tree's days in the sun. It reminds us never to give up adventure. To take the risk of growing and, rather than becoming root bound, to let our roots grow deep in God's love. It reminds us to lift our marriage branches toward heaven and let the storms of life continue to challenge us to grow closer to each other.

We met Carlos and Genie at our church's mission conference. Their enthusiasm, energy, and sheer joy of living drew us to them. Parents of two young daughters and missionaries in Mexico, they were interested in helping marriages and families. They were especially fascinated with our concept of "Marriage Supper Clubs."

"When we get back to Mexico," Carlos told us, "we will start our own Marriage Supper Club." Assuring us they would stay in touch, we said goodbye, looking forward to hearing from them in the future.

So you can imagine our shock when the next November we received a letter from Carlos telling us that Genie had died suddenly of meningitis. Now, his life was turned upside down. He was alone with his two young daughters.

As our mission conference rolled around that spring, we wondered if Carlos would be there. He was, and he sent word that he wanted to talk with us. We'll never forget that conversation.

Carlos told us how he and Genie started their own Supper Club and how they kept each others' children so each couple could have dates. It really worked! Their dates were fun, refreshing, and reenergizing for their marriages. Then he told us about the last week of Genie's life.

"That week it was our time for others to keep our children. So on Sunday we had a great date. We walked and talked and just enjoyed being together. The next day I left for an out-of-town conference. When I kissed Genie goodbye, I had no clue it would be the last time I would hold her in my arms. Soon after I left, she became ill and in a matter of hours she was gone.

See each morning as if it were the morning of the very first day; treasure each day as if it were the evening of the very last day.

ANONYMOUS

"Tell other couples," Carlos told us with his voice breaking, "not to take each other for granted, to seize the day, to take time for their marriages now. You just don't know how long you will have with each other."

Then Carlos added, "The one comfort I have, even though I miss Genie dreadfully, is that we did take time for our own marriage. I can live my life with no regrets."

Our eyes filled with tears. We thought of the past week. We had been busy. Too busy. We had missed our weekly date. Then we heard God whisper to us . . . *Seize the day for your marriage! Not*

Quiet Whispers from God's Heart for Couples

*tomorrow, not next week,
next month or next year!
Seize the day today!*

Fortunately, this story
has a happy ending. Carlos
came back to the United
States with his two
daughters. Time heals.
Life goes on. Sandy,
another missionary who
also had a
burden for Mexico,
entered his life. Love
blossomed. Now, back
in Mexico, Carlos and
Sandy are partners in
marriage and ministry
and parents to the two
girls. They have regular
dates. They work at keep-
ing their own
relationship growing
and fresh. They keep
on "seizing the day"!
Can we do less? Heaven
forbid, but it could
be all that we have!

Rose poured another cup of coffee. "Maybe the caffeine will kick in soon," she mumbled to herself. The hectic weekend was over, and here she was facing another Monday morning—another week of being both mom and dad to her three preschool boys. Not exactly the way she and Kent had pictured family life years ago, when the greatest crisis was how to make it through the month on their meager budget.

Finances were no longer the major stresser in their marriage. Instead, the present stress was Kent's job. Being a successful marketing consultant required Kent to be an absentee dad and husband for most of the week, Monday through Friday. The next rung on Kent's career ladder should require less travel, but for now, extensive traveling was just part of the landscape.

Rose thought of Kent. This morning he had slipped out early before she woke up. She didn't even get to kiss him good-bye. Now he was somewhere in the sky between Dallas and Los Angeles and would not return until Friday when another whirlwind weekend would greet them. Then the cycle would repeat itself. And just as the boys readjusted to having Dad home again, the weekend would be gone and Kent would head for the airport.

Rose loved being a mom. She realized that life is lived in seasons, that now was her opportunity to impact these young lives. She also loved Kent, but as she faced another week as a single parent, she was discouraged and felt so alone. How can I make it through another week? She honestly didn't know. Then she felt God's unmistakable presence and His assurance, *You can make it through this week one moment at a time. You are not alone. I am with you. Life is lived in moments. Trust Me to give you the strength and courage for this time in your life. I have called you to love and nurture your children and to partner with Kent. Together you can surmount the challenges of this season of your lives.*

The Lord gives strength to his people; the Lord blesses his people with peace.

PSALMS 29:11

Slowly, as Rose sipped her coffee, she reminded herself, *this crazy schedule is just for a season. Kent's traveling won't go on forever. The boys will grow up. I can choose to live moment-by-moment, to love and nurture our sons, and to love and support Kent. Our love can deepen through partnering together even with miles between us.*

Her thoughts were interrupted by a gentle tug on her bathrobe. "Mommy, will you read me a book?"

Billy, her oldest son, looked up at her expectantly. "Sure I will," she replied. Billy threw his arms around her, and in that hug she discovered the energy she needed for the moment.

Then she realized, her Heavenly Father would provide the strength for every future moment—for this day, this week, and the weeks to come.

You'll have to check your luggage in at the airline counter inside," the curb-side porter said.

Another cancelled flight. Another delay. Exhausted after leading a weekend seminar, we were very ready to get home. We looked at each other and sighed. "Are we having fun yet?" Dave asked.

Fun wasn't exactly how I (Claudia) would describe this rather frustrating situation. Besides, it was my birthday, and I wanted to celebrate it at home. Now we were going to be several hours late getting there.

Unfortunately, airport delays are all too familiar for us. Leading seminars several weekends each month, cancelled and delayed flights just come with our job. But that day it was more exasperating because it was my birthday. I was tired and just wanted to go home.

Finally we boarded another flight . . . and sat alone. On top of everything else, they couldn't give us seats together. I silently asked, "Why today, of all days?"

Then just as the plane started racing down the runway I heard an almost audible answer, *Why not today?* Then silence.

"Because it's my birthday! I want to get home!" I silently argued.

The whisper continued, *If life were totally predictable—totally on schedule—think how boring it would be! Delays, change of plans, and cancellations are part of the fabric of life. My child, relax. Trust Me. I hold the master plan for your life. Flights can and will be cancelled and delayed, but I will never be late or forsake you. Trust Me with your life . . . trust Me with your marriage . . . trust Me today with your birthday.*

Be strong and courageous. Do not be terrified; do not be discouraged, for the Lord your God will be with you wherever you go.

JOSHUA 1:9

The plane left the ground and climbed through the clouds into the brilliant rays of the sun. I pushed the seat recliner button, put my head back, and relaxed. If airport delays were just part of life, perhaps I should embrace them. After all, the flight, though a rescheduled one, was taking us home.

Soon Dave and I would be sitting side-by-side on our screened porch. There would be plenty of time to celebrate our unpredictable—and definitely not boring—life, to celebrate our marriage, and at long last, to celebrate my birthday. I decided to relax. After all . . . I would have a whole year to be fifty-seven!

Side by side, hand in hand, we walk along the beach. We're not exactly dressed for the beach. Having just completed a six-hour marriage conference, we desperately need some down time-time to kick back and relax—but we forgot our jeans. What was that about our "all work and no play" mentality? Recently didn't one of our sons tell us to "get a life"? Here we are at one of the most beautiful beaches in Florida, and we didn't even think about packing beach clothes. Not to worry. We simply kicked off our shoes and rolled up our slacks. Now relaxing, we're walking on the beach.

The tide's coming in and chasing us as we try not to get wet. Before long our guard slips. The waves win. Our slacks are now wet and sandy. No need for further concern. We relax. Beaches do that to us. It's as if our eyes and ears are opened . . . and our hearts. We pause to appreciate the rolling waves, the sea gulls flying above. The birds standing on one leg. Other lovers passed by. At times like this, life slows down. We stop. Our eyes lock. We kiss. We look at each other through the filter of so many years of being soul mates, companions, lovers.

And then we see her. Lily, our delightful twelve-month-old granddaughter. Lily sees the beach for the very first time. The glee. The delight. Her parents revel in the wonder of it all. Our son and daughter-in-law, here to help with our conference, are in their jeans and T-shirts—much better prepared for the beach than we are. As we reflect on this young couple we realize they are also better prepared to be parents. Better prepared to build a marriage. And then, it was as if we heard an audible whisper, we realize that . . . *life goes forward, not backwards . . . and just as constant as the sands of time, our Heavenly Father goes forward with us. Just as constant as the waves of the ocean, His love will always encompass us.*

We think of our sons, their wives, and our grandchildren, including precious Lily. Yet, even now I remember my parents, in years gone by, walking on the beach, hand in hand. Kissing. Then I was the child. Today, I'm the husband, the dad, the granddad. Life goes forward.

We pause and together we pray, *"Please let us be a positive marriage model for our children and grandchildren. May we leave a path of healthy relationships for them to follow in the sands of time."*

GOD'S QUIET WHISPERS TO US

....

....

....

....

....

....

....

....

....

....

....

....

....

....

GOD'S QUIET WHISPERS TO US

....

....

....

....

....

....

....

....

....

....

....

....

....

....

....

....

....

....

....

....

....

....

....

....

....

....

....

....

....

....

....

....

....

....

....

....

....

....

....

....

....

....

GOD'S QUIET WHISPERS TO US

....

....

....

....

....

....

....

....

....

....

....

....

....

....